Table of Contents

Introduction

Unveiling the Pathway to Entrepreneurial Success in "From Zero to Profit"

Embarking on the entrepreneurial journey is a thrilling yet challenging endeavor that often begins with a vision, an idea, or a desire to make a difference in the world of business. "From Zero to Profit" stands as a guiding beacon for aspiring entrepreneurs and business enthusiasts alike, offering a comprehensive roadmap to navigate the intricate terrain from conceptualization to profitability. This book encapsulates the essence of entrepreneurial spirit, encapsulating the collective wisdom, strategies, and practical insights essential for transforming innovative concepts into thriving, profitable ventures.

The genesis of any successful business rests on the foundation of a resilient and visionary mindset. Aspiring entrepreneurs frequently grapple with questions that revolve around where to start, how to identify opportunities, and what it takes to bring ideas to fruition. This book is crafted as a mentor, a companion that addresses these fundamental queries and encourages readers to embrace the entrepreneurial mindset. It champions the virtues of resilience, adaptability, and a forward-thinking approach essential to surmount the challenges encountered on the path to success.

At its core, "From Zero to Profit" is a testament to the transformative power of ideas. It emphasizes that no idea is too small or too grand, nurturing readers' creative instincts and empowering them to shape their raw concepts into viable business propositions. By providing a step-by-step approach, the book aids in refining and validating ideas, guiding readers through the crucial process of market research and analysis. It sheds light on deciphering market trends, understanding consumer behavior, and identifying unmet needs – all integral components for laying the groundwork for a successful business.

Crucial to the entrepreneurial journey is the blueprint that sets the course for the entire venture – the business plan. "From Zero to Profit" places great emphasis on the art of crafting a robust business plan. This indispensable tool serves as a strategic compass, outlining goals, strategies, financial projections, and operational frameworks. The book offers comprehensive guidance on creating compelling business plans that resonate with potential investors, partners, and stakeholders, setting the stage for execution and growth.

Transitioning from ideation to execution, the book meticulously guides readers through the practicalities of establishing and managing a business. It navigates through the labyrinth of administrative tasks, legal considerations, and financial prerequisites involved in setting up a business entity. From choosing the most suitable legal structure to initiating financial systems and processes, each intricate step is unveiled, empowering readers to maneuver through these initial hurdles with confidence.

The significance of branding and establishing a unique brand identity cannot be overstated in the competitive business landscape. "From Zero to Profit" dedicates substantial attention to this aspect, highlighting the pivotal role of branding in attracting customers, fostering brand loyalty, and differentiating businesses from competitors. Readers are encouraged to craft compelling brand stories that resonate with their target audience, fostering emotional connections and trust.

Moving beyond inception, the book delves into the realms of marketing and sales strategies – indispensable components for business growth and sustainability. It navigates readers through the intricacies of formulating effective marketing plans, leveraging digital platforms, and harnessing the power of social media and online presence to expand reach and engagement. Furthermore, it delves into the art of salesmanship, equipping readers with persuasive techniques to convert leads into loyal customers.

Operational efficiency and effective team management are pivotal for a business's success. "From Zero to Profit" imparts valuable insights into recruiting the right talent, streamlining day-to-day operations, and fostering a customer-centric approach. As businesses scale, the book offers guidance on maintaining quality standards, optimizing workflow, and nurturing a positive work culture conducive to growth.

Financial literacy and astuteness form the bedrock of sustainable business growth. This book provides a comprehensive understanding of financial management, encompassing budgeting, financial planning, cash flow management, and strategies for enhancing profitability. It equips readers with the tools to make informed financial decisions and navigate the complexities of funding and investment.

Beyond immediate profitability, "From Zero to Profit" illuminates the path to sustainability and long-term success. It champions sustainable business practices, advocating for ethical approaches that contribute positively to society and the environment. The book also emphasizes the importance of innovation, adaptability to industry trends, and the foresight needed to envision a future where businesses not only thrive but also leave a lasting legacy.

In its essence, "From Zero to Profit" is not merely a book; it's a compendium of knowledge, experience, and wisdom curated to guide aspiring entrepreneurs through the labyrinth of uncertainties toward the beacon of success. With real-world examples, case studies, actionable strategies, and practical exercises, this book becomes an indispensable companion, empowering readers to embark on their entrepreneurial odyssey with confidence, resilience, and a clear vision of turning dreams into profitable realities.

Chapter 1

Understanding the Entrepreneurial Mindset

Introduction to Entrepreneurial Mindset

The journey from an idea to a profitable business is not solely about executing plans; it begins with cultivating the right mindset. This chapter serves as a foundational cornerstone, emphasizing the significance of the entrepreneurial mindset in shaping successful ventures.

- **The Essence of Entrepreneurial Thinking**

Entrepreneurial thinking encapsulates a mindset characterized by innovation, resilience, creativity, and a visionary approach towards problem-solving. It's a way of thinking that transcends traditional boundaries, embracing uncertainty as an opportunity rather than a deterrent. At its core, entrepreneurial thinking embodies a unique blend of traits and practices that drive individuals to identify opportunities, take calculated risks, and create value in an ever-evolving landscape.

Innovation stands tall as the cornerstone of entrepreneurial thinking. Entrepreneurs possess a keen eye for spotting gaps in the market, unmet needs, or inefficient processes. They thrive on turning these insights into innovative solutions, whether it's a disruptive product, service, or an entirely new business model. This mindset encourages a continuous cycle of ideation, iteration, and adaptation, fostering an environment ripe for groundbreaking advancements.

Resilience is an inherent trait deeply embedded in entrepreneurial thinking. The journey from idea conception to actualizing a profitable business is fraught with challenges, setbacks, and failures. Entrepreneurs understand the inevitability of obstacles and setbacks but approach them as learning opportunities. Their ability to pivot, bounce back from failures, and persist in the face of adversity is what sets them apart. This resilience fuels their determination to pursue their vision despite the odds stacked against them.

Creativity is another hallmark of entrepreneurial thinking. Entrepreneurs possess the ability to think outside the box, envisioning possibilities where others might see limitations. They combine disparate ideas, concepts, and perspectives to generate innovative solutions. Creativity fuels the ideation process, enabling entrepreneurs to develop unique value propositions that resonate with their target audience.

Visionary thinking is the guiding force behind every entrepreneurial endeavor. Entrepreneurs possess a clear and compelling vision of the future they wish to create. They are adept at forecasting trends, anticipating shifts in the market, and envisioning opportunities that others might overlook. This forward-thinking perspective allows entrepreneurs to set ambitious goals, create long-term strategies, and navigate their ventures toward success.

Adaptability and agility are crucial facets of entrepreneurial thinking. In a dynamic and ever-changing business landscape, the ability to adapt swiftly to market shifts, consumer preferences, and technological advancements is paramount. Entrepreneurs embrace change as an opportunity for growth, remaining flexible and open-minded to pivot their strategies when necessary.

Entrepreneurial thinking thrives on calculated risk-taking. While risk aversion is a natural instinct for many, entrepreneurs embrace calculated risks. They analyze potential risks, weigh them against potential rewards, and make informed decisions that propel their ventures forward. This calculated risk-taking mentality allows entrepreneurs to step outside their comfort zones and explore uncharted territories, often leading to significant breakthroughs.

In conclusion, entrepreneurial thinking embodies a unique mindset that combines innovation, resilience, creativity, visionary thinking, adaptability, and calculated risk-taking. It's a mindset that fuels progress, drives innovation, and propels individuals to turn ideas into impactful ventures. Embracing entrepreneurial thinking fosters a culture of continuous growth, innovation, and value creation, enabling individuals to navigate challenges and capitalize on opportunities in an ever-evolving business landscape.

- **Embracing Risk and Failure**

In the exhilarating pursuit from zero to profit, one of the defining elements marking the path of an entrepreneur is their ability to embrace risk and confront failure head-on. In the dynamic world of business, where uncertainties loom large and challenges are an inherent part of the landscape, a mindset attuned to embracing risks and learning from failures becomes a crucial asset.

Risk, often seen as a deterrent to many, is the cornerstone of entrepreneurial endeavors. It's the audacious step taken into the unknown, the leap of faith that propels a business idea forward. Entrepreneurs who embark on this transformative journey acknowledge that risk is an inseparable companion, an element that brings opportunities to innovate, evolve, and create new pathways to success.

From the inception of an idea to the execution of a business plan, entrepreneurs are required to navigate uncharted territories, make bold decisions, and take calculated risks. It's in these moments of uncertainty that true innovation thrives, as they push boundaries and challenge conventional norms. Embracing risk doesn't mean acting recklessly; rather, it involves strategic planning, informed decision-making, and a willingness to step out of the comfort zone.

However, along the trajectory of entrepreneurship, failures are inevitable companions to risk-taking. Yet, failures are not endpoints; they are stepping stones toward growth and eventual success. Each failure holds valuable lessons, providing invaluable insights that can refine strategies, fortify resilience, and nurture a culture of continuous learning.

The ability to adapt and pivot in the face of failure is what distinguishes successful entrepreneurs. They view setbacks as opportunities for introspection, recalibration, and improvement. Failure becomes a catalyst for innovation, spurring the exploration of alternative approaches and refining business models.

"From Zero to Profit" advocates not just the acceptance but the celebration of failure as a natural part of the entrepreneurial journey. It emphasizes the importance of fostering a supportive environment that encourages risk-taking and embraces failures as invaluable learning experiences. Entrepreneurs are urged to wear their failures as badges of honor, acknowledging that each stumble contributes to their growth and eventual triumph.

Moreover, the book offers insights into risk management strategies, encouraging entrepreneurs to identify, assess, and mitigate risks while remaining agile in their responses. It emphasizes the significance of resilience and perseverance, nurturing a mindset that perceives challenges as opportunities for innovation and growth.

Ultimately, "Embracing Risk and Failure: From Zero to Profit" is not merely a mantra; it's a guiding philosophy that shapes the entrepreneurial spirit. It's about accepting the uncertainty, leveraging it to fuel creativity, and persisting in the face of adversity. By acknowledging risk and embracing failure, entrepreneurs unlock their potential to innovate, grow, and transform their dreams into profitable realities.

- **Vision and Adaptability**

Vision and adaptability are two cornerstones that define the success of individuals, organizations, and even societies. In the landscape of personal growth, business endeavors, and societal evolution, the synergy between having a clear vision and the flexibility to adapt is paramount.

At the heart of any significant achievement lies a compelling vision. It serves as a guiding beacon, illuminating the path toward a desired future state. A vision encapsulates aspirations, values, and goals, providing a sense of purpose and direction. Individuals or organizations with a strong vision possess a magnetic force that rallies people, resources, and efforts toward a shared objective.

A well-defined vision isn't confined to mere ambitions; it's a vivid picture that inspires action, fuels innovation, and propels progress. It empowers individuals to transcend the status quo, encouraging them to dream big, think creatively, and set audacious yet attainable goals. Visionaries, whether in business or society, possess the foresight to anticipate trends, identify opportunities, and steer efforts toward a future they envision.

However, a vision, no matter how meticulously crafted, encounters the unpredictable terrain of reality. This is where adaptability becomes the vital companion to vision. Adaptability is the art of responding to change, uncertainty, and unforeseen challenges with resilience, agility, and a willingness to evolve.

In a dynamic and ever-evolving world, rigid adherence to a predefined vision without room for adaptation can lead to stagnation or failure. Adaptability is the ability to pivot, recalibrate strategies, and embrace change while staying true to the core vision. It's about acknowledging shifts in the environment, market demands, or societal trends and making proactive adjustments without compromising the ultimate goal.

Vision without adaptability is akin to sailing without adjusting the sails to changing winds. The most successful leaders and organizations understand the delicate balance between staying anchored to a compelling vision and being nimble enough to navigate through turbulent waters. They demonstrate the courage to embrace change, learn from failures, and pivot swiftly when circumstances demand.

Moreover, adaptability fosters innovation. It encourages experimentation, fosters a culture of continuous improvement, and promotes learning from both successes and setbacks. Adaptability enables individuals and organizations to leverage newfound insights, refine strategies, and capitalize on emerging opportunities that align with the overarching vision.

History is replete with examples of visionary leaders and innovative organizations that have thrived due to their adaptability. Companies that have endured the test of time often attribute their success not just to their initial vision but to their ability to adapt to market shifts and evolving consumer needs.

In conclusion, vision and adaptability are not opposing forces; rather, they are complementary facets essential for sustainable growth and success. A robust vision provides direction and purpose, while adaptability empowers the agility needed to navigate the ever-changing landscape. Together, they form a dynamic synergy that propels individuals, businesses, and societies toward greater heights, ensuring relevance and resilience in an ever-evolving world.

- **Cultivating a Growth Mindset**

Cultivating a growth mindset is a transformative approach centered on embracing challenges, persisting in the face of setbacks, and seeing failures as opportunities for learning and improvement. It involves believing that abilities can be developed through dedication and hard work, fostering resilience and innovation. Individuals with a growth mindset view obstacles as stepping stones to success, seeking opportunities for growth and development. By valuing effort, seeking constructive feedback, and embracing continuous learning, they cultivate a mindset that fuels personal and professional advancement. This mindset shift unlocks potential, fosters resilience, and empowers individuals to achieve greater success in all aspects of life.

- **Passion, Persistence, and Resilience**

Passion, persistence, and resilience are the triumvirate pillars that form the bedrock of success in any endeavor. They embody the spirit of unwavering commitment, determination, and fortitude essential for overcoming challenges and achieving aspirations.

At the heart of this trinity lies passion—the driving force that ignites the flames of ambition and fuels the pursuit of dreams. It is the profound love and enthusiasm for a goal or vision that propels individuals forward, inspiring unwavering dedication and wholehearted engagement. Passion infuses endeavors with purpose, infusing every action with enthusiasm and a sense of fulfillment, transcending obstacles and fueling perseverance in the face of adversity.

Persistence, the relentless pursuit of goals despite setbacks and hurdles, is the force that transforms aspirations into reality. It encompasses the willingness to endure setbacks, learn from failures, and continue forward, undeterred by challenges. It's the refusal to surrender to obstacles, the determination to keep pushing forward, and the commitment to adapt strategies until success is achieved.

Resilience, the ability to bounce back from setbacks, setbacks, and hardships, is the armor that shields one's journey toward success. It embodies adaptability, strength, and mental toughness in the face of adversity. Resilience empowers individuals to weather storms, learn from failures, and emerge stronger, more determined, and better equipped to navigate future challenges.

Together, these three attributes form an indomitable force, guiding individuals through the peaks and valleys of their endeavors. They are the beacon of hope, the driving force that separates triumph from defeat, and the cornerstone upon which extraordinary achievements are built. Embracing passion, persistence, and resilience paves the way for greatness, unlocking the door to boundless opportunities and transforming aspirations into triumphant realities.

- **The Importance of Networking and Collaboration**

Networking and collaboration are cornerstones of success in today's interconnected business landscape, wielding immense importance across industries and professions. Both concepts intertwine to create a synergy that fosters growth, learning, and innovation.

At its core, networking is the art of building and nurturing relationships. It transcends mere social interactions and holds the power to open doors to new opportunities, forge meaningful connections, and cultivate a robust support system. Whether in-person or through digital platforms, networking enables professionals to exchange ideas, share knowledge, and create alliances that transcend geographical boundaries.

One of the primary benefits of networking lies in the access it provides to a diverse pool of resources and expertise. Through networking channels, individuals can tap into a wealth of information, gaining insights and perspectives that can spark innovation and problem-solving. Collaborative partnerships emerge from these connections, enabling individuals or businesses to leverage complementary strengths and skills, leading to mutually beneficial outcomes.

Collaboration, on the other hand, embodies the collective effort of individuals or entities working together towards a common goal. It amplifies the potential for success by pooling together varied talents, experiences, and perspectives. Collaboration not only fosters creativity but also enhances efficiency and productivity by leveraging the strengths of each participant.

In today's dynamic and fast-paced business environment, collaboration is essential for staying competitive. By collaborating with others, businesses can harness collective intelligence, share risks, and access markets that might have been otherwise inaccessible. Moreover, collaboration fuels innovation by encouraging the cross-pollination of ideas and methodologies.

Networking and collaboration complement each other seamlessly. Strong networks facilitate collaboration by connecting like-minded individuals or organizations with shared objectives. Collaborative efforts, in turn, reinforce networks by solidifying relationships and opening doors to new connections.

In essence, the symbiotic relationship between networking and collaboration forms the backbone of success in the modern professional landscape. They foster an environment where expertise is shared, creativity is amplified, and opportunities for growth are maximized. By recognizing and harnessing the power of networking and collaboration, individuals and businesses can propel themselves towards greater achievements and sustainable success.

- **Balancing Ambition and Realism**

Balancing ambition and realism is the cornerstone of sustainable success in any endeavor. Ambition fuels our aspirations, ignites creativity, and propels us toward our goals. It's the driving force behind innovation and progress, pushing us to dream big and reach for the stars. However, when tempered with realism, ambition becomes more than mere enthusiasm—it becomes a practical roadmap.

Realism grounds our ambitions by providing a clear lens through which we assess challenges, limitations, and feasibility. It prompts us to set achievable milestones, consider risks, and adapt our strategies to navigate obstacles effectively. Finding equilibrium between these forces involves setting audacious yet attainable goals, embracing calculated risks, and remaining adaptable to change.

A harmonious blend of ambition and realism allows for strategic planning, prudent decision-making, and agile adjustments when needed. It fosters a mindset that embraces big ideas while acknowledging the practical steps necessary to transform those visions into tangible, sustainable achievements. Ultimately, this balance empowers individuals to pursue their ambitions with confidence, purpose, and a pragmatic approach.

Conclusion

Understanding the entrepreneurial mindset is the cornerstone of a successful journey from zero to profit. This chapter equips readers with the foundational principles, insights, and exercises necessary to cultivate and embody the entrepreneurial mindset. By embracing vision, adaptability, resilience, and a growth-oriented perspective, aspiring entrepreneurs are primed to embark on a transformative journey towards building profitable and sustainable businesses.

Chapter 2

Identifying Profitable Opportunities

In the world of entrepreneurship, the ability to identify and capitalize on profitable opportunities stands as the cornerstone of success. This pivotal chapter within "From Zero to Profit" focuses on honing the skill of recognizing viable and lucrative prospects that form the bedrock of a thriving business.

- **Understanding Market Dynamics**

At the heart of identifying profitable opportunities lies a deep understanding of market dynamics. Entrepreneurs must analyze trends, consumer behavior, and industry shifts to unearth potential niches or underserved markets. This chapter meticulously outlines methodologies for conducting comprehensive market research. It delves into the importance of gathering data, interpreting market trends, and studying competitors to identify gaps waiting to be filled.

- **Recognizing Unmet Needs**

Successful entrepreneurs possess a keen eye for identifying unmet needs within the market. Whether it's solving existing problems more efficiently or introducing innovative solutions, this chapter guides readers on how to spot these gaps. It encourages creative thinking and challenges individuals to think outside the box, sparking ideas that could potentially revolutionize industries.

- **Assessing Demand and Feasibility**

Identifying opportunities goes hand in hand with assessing the demand and feasibility of a potential business venture. This chapter explores methods to gauge demand, conduct surveys, and validate ideas. It emphasizes the importance of feasibility studies, ensuring that identified opportunities align with an entrepreneur's resources, capabilities, and long-term vision.

- **Leveraging Emerging Trends**

Staying ahead in the entrepreneurial landscape requires a keen observation of emerging trends. This chapter enlightens readers on the art of spotting these trends, be it technological advancements, changing consumer preferences, or societal shifts. By identifying and capitalizing on these trends, entrepreneurs can position themselves strategically, fostering innovation and staying competitive.

- **Innovating and Disrupting Markets**

Innovation is a driving force behind profitable opportunities. This chapter encourages entrepreneurs to embrace innovation, fostering a mindset that challenges conventional thinking. It explores ways to disrupt existing markets or create entirely new ones by introducing groundbreaking products, services, or business models.

- **Evaluating Risk and Reward**

No opportunity comes without risks, and evaluating these risks against potential rewards is crucial. This chapter equips readers with frameworks for risk assessment and mitigation strategies. It encourages calculated risk-taking while emphasizing the need for thorough analysis and contingency planning.

- **Case Studies and Real-Life Examples**

To illustrate the concepts discussed, this chapter offers a plethora of real-life case studies and examples. These narratives showcase how successful entrepreneurs identified opportunities, navigated challenges, and turned their visions into profitable ventures. From startups disrupting industries to established businesses adapting to changing landscapes, these stories inspire and provide invaluable insights.

- **Practical Exercises and Actionable Steps**

Moreover, "From Zero to Profit" doesn't merely impart knowledge but also engages readers through practical exercises and actionable steps. These exercises are designed to stimulate critical thinking, encourage idea generation, and guide individuals in applying the concepts discussed directly to their own entrepreneurial aspirations.

Conclusion

Chapter 2 serves as a foundational pillar in the entrepreneurial journey, guiding readers to view the business landscape through a lens of opportunity and innovation. By mastering the art of identifying profitable opportunities, aspiring entrepreneurs are better equipped to lay the groundwork for sustainable and successful ventures, setting the stage for the chapters that follow in their journey "From Zero to Profit."

Chapter 3

Crafting Your Business Idea

- **Understanding the Ideation Process**

The chapter commences by demystifying the ideation process. It elucidates the importance of creativity and innovation in generating business ideas. It explores techniques to spark creativity, brainstorm effectively, and think outside the box. Emphasizing the need to identify problems or unmet needs, readers are guided through methodologies like design thinking, problem-solving frameworks, and ideation exercises to generate unique and feasible business concepts.

- **Identifying Your Passion and Strengths**

A significant portion of the chapter is dedicated to helping individuals align their business ideas with their passions and strengths. Readers are encouraged to introspect, identify their interests, skills, and areas of expertise. Through exercises and reflective prompts, they discover how to leverage their unique strengths to create a business idea that resonates personally and professionally.

- **Market Analysis and Validation**

Crafting a business idea necessitates a thorough understanding of the market landscape. This section dives into the importance of market analysis and validation. Readers learn how to conduct market research, analyze trends, study competitors, and assess demand for their proposed product or service. Techniques such as SWOT analysis, market surveys, and prototype testing are explored to validate the viability of the business idea.

- **Refinement and Adaptation**

Refinement is a key phase in the evolution of any business idea. The chapter elucidates strategies to refine and adapt concepts based on feedback and market insights. It discusses the significance of iteration, continuous improvement, and agility in refining the business idea to better align with market needs and customer preferences.

- **Conceptualization of a Unique Value Proposition**

Central to crafting a business idea is the development of a unique value proposition (UVP). This section illuminates the process of defining a UVP that sets the business apart from competitors. Readers learn how to articulate the value their product or service offers to customers, addressing pain points and fulfilling unmet needs effectively.

- **Assessing Feasibility and Sustainability**

Ensuring the feasibility and sustainability of a business idea is imperative. This part of the chapter guides readers in evaluating the feasibility of their concepts, considering factors such as resources required, scalability, potential challenges, and long-term viability. Strategies for risk assessment, contingency planning, and resource allocation are discussed to enhance the chances of success.

Conclusion

Chapter 3 concludes by emphasizing the iterative nature of crafting a business idea. It encourages readers to embrace flexibility, resilience, and an open-minded approach throughout the ideation process. By amalgamating creativity, market insights, passion, and feasibility considerations, this chapter empowers readers to craft business ideas that have the potential to thrive in the competitive business landscape.

Chapter 4

Market Research and Analysis

What is Market Research?

Market research refers to the systematic process of gathering, analyzing, and interpreting data related to a specific market, its consumers, competitors, and broader industry trends. It serves as a crucial tool for businesses to make informed decisions and mitigate risks by understanding customer preferences, demands, and the competitive environment.

Importance of Market Research

1. Identifying Opportunities:

Market research unveils untapped opportunities. It allows businesses to identify gaps in the market, emerging trends, and unmet needs that can be leveraged to create innovative products or services.

2. Understanding Consumer Behavior:

By comprehensively studying consumer behavior, preferences, and buying patterns, businesses can tailor their offerings to meet customer expectations, thus gaining a competitive edge.

3. Assessing Competition:

Analyzing competitors' strengths, weaknesses, strategies, and market positioning provides invaluable insights. This information aids in devising effective differentiation strategies and refining market positioning.

4. Mitigating Risks:

Market research minimizes risks associated with business decisions by providing a data-driven understanding of market dynamics, potential challenges, and industry shifts.

Types of Market Research

1. Primary Research:

This involves collecting firsthand data directly from consumers or the market. Techniques like surveys, interviews, focus groups, and observations are utilized to gather specific information tailored to the research objectives.

2. Secondary Research:

Secondary research involves the analysis of existing data, reports, industry publications, and market studies. It provides a broader perspective and serves as a foundation for primary research by offering context and insights.

Market Analysis

Market analysis involves interpreting gathered data to derive actionable insights. It encompasses various aspects:

1. Industry Analysis:

Understanding the broader industry landscape, trends, regulations, and market size assists in gauging the business's potential within that particular sector.

2. Customer Segmentation:

Segmenting customers based on demographics, psychographics, behaviors, and preferences enables businesses to tailor their marketing strategies and offerings more effectively.

3. Competitor Analysis:

Evaluating competitors' strategies, market share, strengths, weaknesses, and innovations aids in devising strategies to stand out in the market.

4. SWOT Analysis:

A SWOT (Strengths, Weaknesses, Opportunities, Threats) analysis helps businesses identify internal strengths and weaknesses, while recognizing external opportunities and threats in the market.

Implementing Market Research Findings

The insights gleaned from market research and analysis inform critical business decisions across various departments:

- **Product Development:** Designing products/services that align with consumer needs and preferences.
- **Marketing Strategy:** Tailoring marketing campaigns and messaging to specific target audiences.
- **Sales and Distribution:** Determining the most effective channels for product distribution.
- **Business Expansion:** Guiding decisions regarding geographical expansion or diversification.

Conclusion

Market research and analysis are not one-time activities; they are ongoing processes crucial for a business's sustained success. In a fast-paced and competitive business environment, leveraging robust market research practices equips businesses with the foresight and agility needed to adapt, innovate, and thrive amidst ever-changing market dynamics.

Chapter 5

Building a Solid Business Plan

A business plan stands as the cornerstone of every successful venture. It's the roadmap, the guiding document that charts the course for a business's journey from conception to reality. Crafting a solid business plan requires meticulous attention to detail, strategic thinking, and a thorough understanding of various facets crucial to the enterprise's success.

The Purpose of a Business Plan

At its core, a business plan serves multiple purposes. It's not merely a document designed to attract investors or secure funding; rather, it's a blueprint that outlines the business's objectives, strategies, operational structure, and financial projections. It encapsulates the entrepreneur's vision, offering a clear path towards achieving goals and milestones.

Key Components of a Business Plan

1. Executive Summary

This section encapsulates the essence of the entire business plan. It provides a concise overview of the business concept, its unique value proposition, target market, financial projections, and goals.

2. Business Description and Vision

Detail the nature of the business, its mission, vision, and core values. Describe the products or services offered and elucidate on what sets them apart from competitors.

3. Market Analysis

Conduct a comprehensive analysis of the industry, market trends, target audience, and competitive landscape. Insight into customer needs and behavior is crucial in this section.

4. Marketing and Sales Strategy

Outline the marketing strategies and tactics planned to reach the target audience. Include pricing strategies, distribution channels, advertising plans, and sales projections.

5. Operational Plan

This section details the day-to-day operations, including production processes, supply chain management, facilities, technology, and staffing requirements.

6. Management and Organizational Structure

Describe the management team's structure, roles, responsibilities, and expertise. Investors often scrutinize this section to evaluate the team's capability to execute the business plan.

7. Financial Projections

Present comprehensive financial forecasts, including income statements, cash flow projections, and balance sheets. Highlight key assumptions and methodologies used for these projections.

8. Funding Requirements

If seeking funding, clearly articulate the capital requirements, the purpose of the funds, and how they will be utilized to achieve business objectives.

The Process of Building a Business Plan

1. Research and Analysis

Gather data, conduct market research, and analyze industry trends. This phase is crucial for understanding the market, identifying opportunities, and assessing risks.

2. Defining the Business Concept

Craft a compelling narrative that articulates the business's purpose, unique selling proposition, and how it addresses market needs.

3. Strategy Development

Formulate robust strategies for marketing, operations, and financial management. Define the sales and distribution channels, pricing models, and operational workflow.

4. Financial Projections

Develop realistic financial projections based on thorough research and analysis. This includes revenue forecasts, expense estimates, and cash flow projections.

5. Writing and Formatting

Present the business plan in a clear, concise, and professional manner. Use a format that aligns with industry standards and investor expectations.

Importance of a Solid Business Plan

1. Roadmap for Success

A well-structured plan provides direction, enabling entrepreneurs to stay focused on their goals and navigate challenges effectively.

2. Attracting Investors and Funding

Investors and lenders rely on business plans to evaluate the viability of a business. A comprehensive plan instills confidence and increases the likelihood of securing funding.

3. Internal Alignment

A shared vision outlined in the business plan fosters alignment among team members, ensuring everyone works towards common goals.

4. Adaptability and Flexibility

While a business plan sets a clear path, it should also allow for flexibility to adapt to changing market conditions and unforeseen challenges.

Conclusion

In conclusion, building a solid business plan is an iterative process that involves extensive research, strategic thinking, and a clear articulation of ideas. It serves as a blueprint that guides entrepreneurs through the complexities of starting and growing a successful business. A well-crafted plan not only attracts investors but also serves as a crucial tool for decision-making and operational excellence, ultimately paving the way for sustained success and growth.

Creating a solid business plan involves a multifaceted approach, considering various aspects crucial to the success of the business. This comprehensive guide aims to provide an in-depth understanding of the key components, process, and significance of a well-structured business plan in steering a business towards its goals.

Chapter 6

Financing Your Venture

In the realm of entrepreneurship, securing financing is often a pivotal step towards turning an idea into a sustainable and profitable business. Whether launching a startup or expanding an existing venture, understanding the various avenues and strategies for financing is paramount. This comprehensive guide aims to explore the multifaceted landscape of financing a venture, outlining key steps, diverse funding sources, and prudent financial management strategies essential for success.

- **Understanding Financial Needs**

Before delving into financing options, it's imperative to assess the financial requirements of your venture. This involves meticulously calculating startup costs, operational expenses, research and development, marketing, staffing, and contingencies. Having a clear grasp of the capital needed at different stages lays the groundwork for effective financial planning and funding strategies.

- **Bootstrapping and Self-Financing**

One of the initial avenues many entrepreneurs explore is self-financing or bootstrapping. This involves utilizing personal savings, liquidating assets, or leveraging credit cards to fund the business. While it offers autonomy and avoids debt, it also entails personal financial risks and might not suffice for larger-scale ventures.

- **Friends and Family**

Entrepreneurs often turn to their inner circle for financial support in the form of loans or investments. Seeking capital from friends and family can be an accessible and flexible option, yet it necessitates transparent communication, clearly defined terms, and a structured repayment plan to avoid straining personal relationships.

- **Angel Investors**

Angel investors are affluent individuals who provide capital in exchange for equity ownership or convertible debt. Beyond financial backing, they often offer mentorship, industry expertise, and networking opportunities. Engaging with angel investors requires a compelling pitch, a scalable business model, and a coherent growth strategy.

- **Venture Capital**

Venture capital firms specialize in investing in high-growth potential startups in exchange for equity. These firms typically invest larger sums of capital and expect substantial returns. Securing venture capital demands a robust business plan, a scalable business model, and a convincing pitch deck.

- **Crowdfunding Platforms**

Crowdfunding platforms like Kickstarter, Indiegogo, or GoFundMe enable entrepreneurs to showcase their projects to a broad audience, raising funds from individual backers in exchange for rewards or early access. Crowdfunding not only provides capital but also validates market interest and builds a community around the product or service.

- **Small Business Loans and Lines of Credit**

Government-backed Small Business Administration (SBA) loans or traditional bank loans offer accessible funding options for entrepreneurs. These loans come with varying interest rates, terms, and collateral requirements. Establishing a strong credit history, presenting a comprehensive business plan, and demonstrating repayment capability are crucial in securing these loans.

- **Grants and Contests**

Numerous grants, competitions, and incubator programs provide non-dilutive funding to startups and innovative ventures. These opportunities often come with mentorship, networking, and visibility benefits. Researching and applying for grants aligned with the business's goals and industry can be a lucrative avenue for funding.

- **Managing Finances Wisely**

Acquiring funding is just the beginning; prudent financial management is vital for the sustained success of any venture. Implementing efficient accounting systems, monitoring cash flow, budgeting meticulously, and optimizing expenses are critical practices to ensure the judicious utilization of funds.

Conclusion

In conclusion, financing a venture demands a multifaceted approach, combining a thorough understanding of the business's financial needs with astute strategies to secure funding. Entrepreneurs must assess the suitability of various financing options, aligning them with the business's growth stage, goals, and industry dynamics. Successful financing not only provides the necessary capital but also opens doors to invaluable resources, guidance, and opportunities essential for a thriving entrepreneurial journey.

Starting Up:

Establishing Your Business

Chapter 7

Choosing the Right Legal Structure

Choosing the right legal structure for your business is a pivotal decision that can significantly impact its operations, liabilities, taxes, and overall success. The legal structure you select will define how your business is organized, managed, and taxed, so it's crucial to understand the various options available and their implications before making this important choice.

Here's a comprehensive exploration of different legal structures and considerations to help you make an informed decision:

1. Sole Proprietorship

A sole proprietorship is the simplest and most common form of business structure. It involves a single individual owning and operating the business. It's easy to set up, offers complete control, and has minimal regulatory requirements. However, the owner is personally liable for all business debts and obligations, which means personal assets could be at risk in case of legal issues or debts incurred by the business.

2. Partnership

Partnerships involve two or more individuals sharing ownership and responsibility for the business. There are two primary types: general partnerships (where all partners share equal responsibility and liability) and limited partnerships (with a mix of general partners, who have unlimited liability, and limited partners, whose liability is restricted to their investment). Partnerships provide shared decision-making, resources, and expertise but also involve shared liabilities and potential conflicts among partners.

3. Limited Liability Company (LLC)

An LLC combines elements of both partnerships and corporations. It offers limited liability protection to its owners (known as members), shielding their personal assets from business liabilities. LLCs provide flexibility in management structure and have fewer formalities compared to corporations. They can choose to be taxed as either a partnership or a corporation, providing tax advantages and operational flexibility.

4. Corporation

Corporations are separate legal entities distinct from their owners (shareholders). They offer the strongest liability protection, as shareholders' personal assets are typically not at risk for business debts or lawsuits. Corporations have a more complex structure, with a board of directors overseeing major decisions, officers managing day-to-day operations, and shareholders owning the company. They also face more extensive regulatory requirements and formalities, such as regular meetings, record-keeping, and annual filings.

Factors to Consider in Choosing the Right Structure:

- **Liability Protection:** Consider the level of personal liability exposure you're willing to accept. Protecting personal assets is a significant factor in choosing a legal structure.
- **Tax Implications:** Different structures have varying tax obligations and benefits. Consult with tax professionals to understand how each structure impacts your tax liabilities and benefits.
- **Cost and Complexity:** Consider the setup costs, ongoing maintenance, and administrative requirements associated with each structure. Some, like sole proprietorships, have minimal costs, while corporations often involve higher setup and maintenance expenses.
- **Ownership and Management:** Determine how much control and decision-making power you want. Some structures, like partnerships, offer shared management, while others, like corporations, have a more hierarchical structure.
- **Future Growth and Funding:** Consider the potential for business growth and the ability to attract investors or raise capital. Certain structures may be more favorable for seeking funding or going public in the future.

- **State Laws and Regulations:** Legal structures are subject to state laws and regulations. Be aware of the specific requirements and regulations in the state where you plan to establish your business.

Conclusion

Choosing the right legal structure is a critical step in laying the foundation for your business. Each structure has its own advantages and drawbacks, and the optimal choice depends on your business goals, risk tolerance, taxation considerations, and long-term vision. Seek advice from legal and financial professionals to make an informed decision that aligns with your business objectives and helps set the stage for sustainable growth and success.

Chapter 8

Registering Your Business

Registering your business marks a pivotal step in the journey from concept to reality. It's the moment when your entrepreneurial vision transitions into a legal entity recognized by authorities. This chapter of "From Zero to Profit" focuses on the crucial aspects of registering a business, elucidating the processes, considerations, and significance of this foundational step.

Understanding Legal Structures: The chapter initiates by elucidating various business structures - sole proprietorship, partnership, limited liability company (LLC), corporation, etc. Each structure comes with its own set of legal implications, tax considerations, and liability frameworks. Readers are guided to choose a structure aligned with their business goals and risk tolerance.

Naming and Branding: A pivotal part of registration involves choosing a business name that resonates with the brand's identity. The chapter offers guidance on selecting a name that is distinctive, memorable, and compliant with legal requirements. It also covers the process of conducting a thorough name search to ensure uniqueness and availability.

Registering with Authorities: Depending on the chosen business structure and location, there are specific government bodies and agencies to register with. This section provides a comprehensive guide on the necessary paperwork, licenses, permits, and registrations required at federal, state, and local levels. It outlines the procedures and timelines for filing documents and obtaining necessary clearances.

Tax Identification and Compliance: Registering a business often involves obtaining an Employer Identification Number (EIN) or Tax Identification Number (TIN). The chapter explains the importance of these identifiers for tax purposes and details the steps to acquire them. Additionally, it sheds light on tax obligations and compliance requirements applicable to different business structures.

Legal Documentation and Agreements: Setting up a business involves drafting legal documents and agreements. This section highlights the significance of operating agreements, partnership agreements, bylaws, and other legal contracts relevant to the chosen business structure. Readers gain insights into the importance of these documents in defining roles, responsibilities, and dispute resolution mechanisms.

Costs and Timelines: Understanding the costs associated with business registration is crucial. This chapter provides a breakdown of potential expenses, such as filing fees, legal consultation costs, and ongoing compliance expenses. Moreover, it offers an overview of the typical timelines involved in the registration process, allowing entrepreneurs to plan effectively.

Post-Registration Obligations: Once the business is registered, there are ongoing compliance requirements. This section outlines annual filings, reporting obligations, and renewal processes that entrepreneurs must adhere to in order to maintain their legal standing and ensure continued operations without interruptions.

"Registering Your Business" in "From Zero to Profit" serves as a comprehensive guide, empowering entrepreneurs to navigate the maze of legalities with confidence. It equips readers with the knowledge and understanding necessary to initiate their business ventures on a solid legal foundation, paving the way for future growth and success.

Chapter 9

Setting Up Financial Systems

In the entrepreneurial journey, establishing robust financial systems stands as a pivotal cornerstone. Chapter 9 navigates through the intricate process of setting up these systems to ensure a business's fiscal health and sustainability. It delves into organizing accounting practices, financial record-keeping, and implementing software tools crucial for efficient financial management.

The chapter primarily focuses on budgeting, cash flow management, and creating financial projections. It outlines methods for monitoring expenses, tracking revenues, and establishing key performance indicators (KPIs) to measure financial progress. Emphasis is placed on the importance of accuracy and transparency in financial reporting to facilitate informed decision-making.

Additionally, the chapter delves into strategies for managing capital, securing funding sources, and understanding the legal and regulatory aspects of financial operations. It educates entrepreneurs on the significance of maintaining financial discipline and implementing checks and balances to mitigate risks.

A thorough understanding of financial systems is crucial for entrepreneurs to make informed strategic decisions, assess business performance, and attract potential investors. The chapter's insights equip entrepreneurs with the necessary tools to create a solid financial foundation, essential for the long-term success and growth of their ventures.

Chapter 10

Creating a Brand Identity

Crafting a distinct and compelling brand identity is pivotal for businesses aiming to stand out in a crowded marketplace. Chapter 10 intricately explores the multifaceted process of developing a brand identity that resonates with the target audience.

This chapter delves into the significance of brand elements such as logos, colors, typography, and brand messaging. It emphasizes the importance of aligning these elements cohesively to communicate the brand's values, personality, and unique selling propositions effectively.

Moreover, the chapter discusses market research techniques to understand consumer behavior and preferences, allowing entrepreneurs to create a brand identity that resonates with their audience. Strategies for brand positioning, differentiation, and storytelling are also elaborated upon, aiding in building an emotional connection with consumers.

Case studies and real-world examples supplement the chapter, illustrating successful brand identity strategies adopted by renowned companies. Entrepreneurs are encouraged to develop a holistic brand strategy that encompasses every touchpoint, ensuring consistency and authenticity across all interactions with consumers.

Overall, Chapter 10 equips entrepreneurs with the knowledge and tools necessary to craft a compelling brand identity, enabling them to create a lasting impression and build a loyal customer base.

Chapter 11

Developing Initial Products/Services

Chapter 11 focuses on the critical stage of conceptualizing, designing, and developing the initial products or services for a new business. It delves into the ideation process, market research, and prototyping necessary to transform ideas into tangible offerings that meet customer needs.

The chapter emphasizes the importance of conducting thorough market research to identify gaps, assess competition, and understand consumer preferences. By leveraging this information, entrepreneurs can tailor their products or services to address specific pain points or provide unique solutions.

Furthermore, the chapter discusses the iterative process of prototyping and testing. It encourages entrepreneurs to gather feedback from potential customers, iterate on designs, and refine their offerings to ensure they align with market demands and expectations.

Additionally, considerations regarding pricing strategies, production processes, and scalability are addressed in this chapter. Entrepreneurs are guided on making informed decisions about the feasibility, cost-effectiveness, and potential profitability of their initial products or services.

By combining strategic planning, market insights, and iterative development processes, Chapter 11 equips entrepreneurs with the necessary framework to create and refine their initial offerings. This enables them to enter the market with products or services that resonate with customers, fostering a strong foundation for business growth and success.

Chapter 12

Understanding Your Target Audience

Understanding your target audience is fundamental in any successful business strategy. It involves gaining insights into the demographics, behaviors, preferences, and needs of the individuals or groups who are most likely to engage with your products or services. By comprehending your audience, you can tailor your marketing efforts more effectively.

This process involves thorough market research, data analysis, and customer segmentation. Demographic factors such as age, gender, location, income, and education level can provide a foundation, but psychographic elements like lifestyle, values, interests, and buying habits offer deeper insights. Employing surveys, interviews, and social media analytics can help gather this information.

By comprehending your audience's pain points and desires, you can create targeted messaging and personalized experiences that resonate with them. This understanding enables the development of products that meet their specific needs and allows for more precise marketing campaigns that reach the right people at the right time with the right message.

Chapter 13

Developing a Marketing Plan

A marketing plan is a roadmap that outlines an organization's marketing strategy, goals, and tactics to achieve those objectives. It integrates market research findings and insights into actionable steps. A well-crafted marketing plan typically includes an analysis of the current market situation, identifies target audiences, establishes measurable goals, and outlines the strategies and tactics to reach those goals.

Key components of a marketing plan include defining the unique selling proposition (USP), determining the marketing mix (product, price, place, promotion), setting a budget, selecting the appropriate marketing channels, and establishing metrics for evaluating success.

Successful marketing plans are adaptable and responsive to changes in the market. They are also focused on consistent messaging across all channels to ensure a unified brand image and customer experience.

Chapter 14

Effective Sales Techniques

Sales techniques encompass the methods, approaches, and skills employed by sales professionals to convert leads into customers. It involves building relationships, understanding customer needs, and persuasively communicating the value proposition of products or services.

Effective sales techniques emphasize active listening, empathy, and problem-solving. Salespeople need to ask insightful questions to uncover customer pain points and offer tailored solutions that address those needs. Building trust and rapport with potential clients is crucial in fostering long-term relationships and securing sales.

Additionally, leveraging storytelling, demonstrating product features, offering trials or samples, and providing exceptional customer service are all part of effective sales techniques. Continuous learning and adapting to different customer personalities and situations are key traits of successful sales professionals.

Chapter 15

Building an Online Presence

In today's digital era, having a robust online presence is imperative for businesses to remain competitive. Building an online presence involves creating and maintaining a digital footprint across various platforms like websites, social media, blogs, and forums.

A website serves as the cornerstone of an online presence, providing information about products or services, contact details, and sometimes even allowing online purchases. Search Engine Optimization (SEO) techniques are crucial to ensure visibility on search engines, driving organic traffic to the website.

Social media platforms offer avenues for engagement, customer interaction, and content distribution. Creating valuable and shareable content tailored to the target audience helps in building brand awareness and fostering a community around the brand.

Chapter 16

Leveraging Social Media for Growth

Social media platforms have become powerful tools for businesses to connect with their audience, build brand awareness, and drive sales. Leveraging social media for growth involves developing a strategy that aligns with business goals and audience preferences across various platforms.

Engagement and interaction are key in social media growth strategies. Consistent posting of relevant content, engaging with the audience through comments and messages, and participating in trending conversations help in increasing visibility and building relationships.

Using analytics tools provided by social media platforms assists in understanding audience behavior, preferences, and the effectiveness of content strategies. Paid advertising on social media can also be employed to reach specific demographics and expand the brand's reach.

Successful social media strategies involve staying updated with platform changes, adapting content to suit different platforms, and maintaining authenticity and consistency in brand messaging across all channels.

Each of these chapters contributes significantly to an organization's overall marketing and sales strategies. Understanding the target audience, developing a robust marketing plan, employing effective sales techniques, building an online presence, and leveraging social media are all essential components in achieving business growth and success in today's competitive landscape.

Chapter 17

Hiring the Right Team

Hiring the right team is a pivotal aspect of any successful business. This chapter delves into the intricacies of assembling a competent and cohesive workforce. It emphasizes the significance of a thorough recruitment process, identifying key skill sets, and assessing cultural fit within the organization.

In this chapter, readers explore various strategies for effective talent acquisition. From crafting compelling job descriptions to conducting rigorous interviews, the focus remains on attracting top-notch candidates who align with the company's values and objectives. Additionally, it covers the importance of diversity in the workplace and how it contributes to innovation and problem-solving.

Understanding the nuances of team dynamics and fostering a collaborative environment is also discussed. Effective team-building techniques, including team retreats, mentorship programs, and ongoing training, are highlighted to enhance productivity and employee satisfaction.

Chapter 18

Managing Day-to-Day Operations

Managing day-to-day operations forms the backbone of a business's success. This chapter provides insights into streamlining processes, optimizing resources, and ensuring smooth functioning across all departments.

Readers are guided through the implementation of efficient systems and protocols to enhance productivity and minimize bottlenecks. The chapter stresses the significance of embracing technology and automation to streamline routine tasks, allowing teams to focus on strategic initiatives.

Additionally, it addresses effective communication strategies within an organization, emphasizing the importance of clarity, transparency, and regular feedback loops. Time management techniques and prioritization methodologies are also explored to enable efficient task execution.

Chapter 19

Optimizing Workflow and Processes

Optimizing workflow and processes is crucial for sustained growth. This chapter offers strategies to evaluate existing workflows, identify inefficiencies, and implement improvements.

Readers learn about various process optimization methodologies such as Lean Six Sigma and Kaizen. The chapter emphasizes the importance of continuous improvement and agility in adapting to market changes.

Furthermore, it discusses the role of data analytics in identifying trends and areas for enhancement. Leveraging technology and analytics tools to gather actionable insights becomes pivotal in refining workflows and enhancing operational efficiency.

Chapter 20

Customer Relationship Management

Customer Relationship Management (CRM) is explored in this chapter as a cornerstone of business success. It highlights the significance of building strong, lasting relationships with customers through personalized experiences and effective communication.

The chapter delves into implementing CRM software and strategies to track customer interactions, gather feedback, and tailor services to meet individual needs. It emphasizes the role of customer feedback in refining products/services and fostering loyalty.

Moreover, it discusses the importance of customer-centricity across all touchpoints, emphasizing the need for a seamless customer journey and the power of word-of-mouth marketing through satisfied customers.

Chapter 21

Scaling Your Business

Scaling a business involves strategic planning and execution to expand operations sustainably. This chapter explores various methods of scaling, including geographic expansion, product diversification, and partnerships/acquisitions.

It emphasizes the significance of scalability in the early stages of business planning and the need to build a robust infrastructure capable of handling growth. Readers gain insights into effective resource allocation, managing increased demand, and maintaining quality standards while scaling.

Furthermore, the chapter covers the challenges and risks associated with scaling, emphasizing the importance of adaptability and agility in responding to market shifts. Strategies for financing growth and accessing new markets are also discussed, providing a comprehensive guide to successfully scale a business while mitigating potential pitfalls.

Financial Management and Growth

Chapter 22

Budgeting and Financial Planning

Budgeting and financial planning are foundational pillars of effective business management. Chapter 22 delves into the significance of creating budgets and devising comprehensive financial plans for businesses of all scales.

A budget serves as a roadmap, guiding businesses in allocating resources, setting goals, and measuring performance. It involves estimating revenues and expenses over a specific period, aiding in informed decision-making. Financial planning extends this by considering long-term objectives, risk management, and capital structure.

Businesses utilize various budgeting techniques like zero-based budgeting, incremental budgeting, or activity-based budgeting. Each method caters to different needs, fostering control and accountability within organizations.

Effective financial planning involves forecasting cash flows, identifying potential risks, and strategizing to mitigate them. It includes assessing current financial health, determining future needs, and aligning resources to achieve objectives.

Embracing technology through budgeting software and financial planning tools streamlines processes, enhances accuracy, and facilitates real-time monitoring, enabling agile adjustments when necessary.

Chapter 23

Managing Cash Flow

Chapter 23 centers on the critical aspect of managing cash flow in business operations. Cash flow, the lifeblood of any enterprise, refers to the movement of cash in and out of a company. It's vital for sustaining day-to-day operations, investing in growth, and meeting financial obligations.

Managing cash flow involves monitoring inflows from sales, investments, or financing and outflows such as expenses, loan repayments, and dividends. Businesses strive to maintain a healthy cash flow by balancing timing discrepancies between inflows and outflows.

Techniques like cash flow forecasting aid in predicting future cash positions, allowing proactive measures to address potential shortfalls. Moreover, optimizing working capital by managing inventory, receivables, and payables assists in enhancing cash flow efficiency.

Businesses employ various strategies to manage cash flow effectively, such as negotiating better payment terms with suppliers, diversifying revenue streams, and having contingency plans for unforeseen circumstances.

Chapter 24

Seeking Investment and Funding

Securing investment and funding is crucial for businesses seeking growth opportunities or starting new ventures. Chapter 24 outlines the processes and strategies involved in acquiring capital to support business objectives.

Businesses explore diverse funding options, including equity financing, debt financing, venture capital, angel investors, crowdfunding, or grants. Each avenue has its advantages and considerations, impacting ownership, risk, and cost of capital.

Preparing a compelling business plan, conducting thorough market research, and presenting a convincing value proposition are vital when seeking investment. Entrepreneurs need to articulate their vision, market potential, and strategies to attract potential investors or lenders.

Establishing credibility, building relationships, and networking within the investment community can open doors to funding opportunities. Businesses should also be mindful of the legal and regulatory aspects associated with different funding sources.

Chapter 25

Profitability and Growth Strategies

Profitability and growth are fundamental objectives for businesses. Chapter 25 delves into the strategies and methodologies employed to achieve sustainable growth while ensuring profitability.

Businesses pursue growth through market expansion, product diversification, mergers, acquisitions, or strategic partnerships. However, sustainable growth necessitates a balance between expansion and maintaining operational efficiency.

Analyzing key performance indicators (KPIs) like return on investment (ROI), profit margins, and customer acquisition costs aids in evaluating profitability and guiding growth strategies. Businesses often engage in continuous innovation, market positioning, and operational optimizations to drive growth.

Additionally, focusing on customer retention, leveraging technology for efficiency gains, and exploring untapped markets are common tactics to fuel growth while safeguarding profitability.

Chapter 26

Adapting to Market Changes

In today's dynamic business landscape, adaptability is paramount for survival and success. Chapter 26 emphasizes the importance of businesses being agile and responsive to market changes and disruptions.

Adapting to market changes involves staying attuned to industry trends, consumer behavior, technological advancements, and regulatory shifts. Businesses need to embrace flexibility in strategies, operations, and offerings to remain competitive.

Employing scenario planning and risk analysis assists in preparing for potential market shifts, enabling businesses to pivot swiftly when necessary. Moreover, fostering a culture of innovation and continuous improvement facilitates adaptability.

Utilizing feedback loops, conducting market research, and engaging with customers enable businesses to gather insights, aiding in informed decision-making and proactive adjustments to changing market dynamics.

In conclusion, Chapters 22 to 26 collectively underscore the significance of prudent financial management, strategic planning, resource allocation, and adaptability in navigating the complexities of modern business environments. Mastering these aspects empowers businesses to not only survive but thrive in an ever-evolving marketplace.

Sustainability and Future Outlook

Chapter 27

Sustainable Business Practices

Sustainable business practices have emerged as a cornerstone of responsible corporate conduct in the modern era. This chapter delves into the multifaceted dimensions of sustainability within the business landscape, encompassing environmental, social, and economic considerations.

Sustainability, fundamentally, involves meeting the needs of the present without compromising the ability of future generations to meet their own needs. In the corporate sphere, this translates into integrating environmentally friendly practices, promoting social responsibility, and ensuring economic viability.

Environmentally, businesses are increasingly recognizing the imperative to reduce their carbon footprint, conserve natural resources, and minimize waste generation. Adopting renewable energy sources, implementing eco-friendly production processes, and embracing circular economy principles are pivotal steps toward environmental sustainability.

Moreover, businesses are under mounting pressure to address social concerns. This encompasses initiatives to support local communities, uphold labor rights, foster diversity and inclusion, and contribute positively to societal well-being. Ethical sourcing, fair labor practices, philanthropic endeavors, and community engagement programs are integral facets of socially responsible business conduct.

Economically, sustainability involves achieving profitability while also considering long-term viability and resilience. This entails prudent financial management, strategic investments in sustainable practices, and balancing short-term gains with long-term objectives.

Companies adopting sustainable practices not only contribute to a healthier planet and society but also often enjoy enhanced brand reputation, customer loyalty, and access to new markets. Nevertheless, challenges persist, including initial investment costs, regulatory complexities, and the need for cultural shifts within organizations.

Chapter 28

Innovating for the Future

Innovation stands as a driving force behind progress and success in the corporate realm. This chapter examines the pivotal role of innovation in shaping the future of businesses, industries, and society at large.

Innovation encompasses a spectrum of activities, from incremental improvements to revolutionary breakthroughs. It involves generating novel ideas, processes, products, or business models that add value, address unmet needs, or disrupt existing markets.

Businesses aiming to innovate must foster a culture that encourages creativity, experimentation, and risk-taking. This culture often thrives in environments where diverse perspectives are welcomed, failure is seen as a learning opportunity, and collaboration is encouraged across departments and disciplines.

Technological advancements, such as artificial intelligence, machine learning, blockchain, and biotechnology, continue to drive innovation across industries. Embracing these technologies enables companies to streamline operations, enhance efficiency, create new products or services, and gain a competitive edge.

Open innovation, partnerships with startups, academia, and other industry players, as well as crowdsourcing ideas, are strategies increasingly employed by forward-thinking organizations to broaden their innovation horizons.

Furthermore, sustainable innovation – which combines environmental and social considerations with novel solutions – is gaining prominence. It involves developing eco-friendly products, implementing green technologies, and devising business models that contribute positively to both society and the environment.

However, navigating innovation comes with challenges, including resource constraints, resistance to change, intellectual property issues, and the need to balance short-term demands with long-term innovation investments.

Chapter 29

Adapting to Industry Trends

Industries are in a constant state of flux, driven by technological advancements, changing consumer behaviors, evolving market dynamics, and global shifts. This chapter explores the importance of adapting to industry trends to remain competitive and relevant.

Staying abreast of industry trends involves vigilance, analysis, and adaptability. Companies must monitor market shifts, consumer preferences, emerging technologies, regulatory changes, and competitive landscapes to identify opportunities and threats.

Digital transformation remains a pervasive trend across industries, reshaping business models, customer experiences, and operational efficiencies. E-commerce, data analytics, Internet of Things (IoT), and cloud computing are just a few aspects driving this transformation.

Moreover, consumer expectations continue to evolve, influencing product development, marketing strategies, and service delivery. Personalization, sustainability, convenience, and ethical considerations increasingly factor into purchasing decisions, prompting businesses to realign their strategies accordingly.

Globalization and geopolitical developments impact supply chains, trade practices, and market access. Businesses must adapt to geopolitical shifts, trade regulations, and geopolitical risks to mitigate disruptions and capitalize on emerging opportunities.

Agility and flexibility are crucial for companies seeking to adapt to industry trends. This often involves fostering a culture of continuous learning, embracing change, and swiftly adjusting strategies in response to market dynamics.

However, challenges persist, including the pace of technological change, competition, regulatory uncertainty, and the need for substantial investments in infrastructure and talent to stay ahead of evolving trends.

Chapter 30

Long-Term Success and Legacy Building

Achieving long-term success goes beyond short-term profits; it involves building a sustainable legacy that transcends generations. This chapter delves into strategies for businesses to secure their future while leaving a positive and enduring impact on society.

Long-term success necessitates a holistic approach that balances financial goals with broader societal and environmental responsibilities. It requires aligning business strategies with core values, ethical principles, and a vision that extends beyond immediate profitability.

Leadership plays a pivotal role in shaping a company's legacy. Leaders who embody a long-term perspective, embrace innovation, foster a culture of inclusivity and sustainability, and prioritize ethical conduct pave the way for enduring success.

Investing in human capital is crucial for sustained success. This involves nurturing talent, providing opportunities for growth and development, fostering a diverse and inclusive workplace culture, and empowering employees to contribute meaningfully to the company's objectives.

Building a legacy also entails actively engaging with stakeholders – customers, employees, communities, investors, and regulators – and addressing their concerns while creating shared value. This involves transparent communication, ethical governance, and a commitment to social and environmental responsibility.

Furthermore, businesses aiming for long-term success must adapt to changing landscapes, anticipate future trends, and continuously innovate. Embracing technological advancements, fostering agility, and being responsive to market shifts are essential components of future-proofing a company.

Ultimately, the pursuit of long-term success and legacy building requires a delicate balance between short-term objectives and enduring values. While challenges such as market volatility, disruptive technologies, and societal expectations persist, businesses that prioritize sustainability, innovation, adaptability, and ethical conduct are better positioned to leave a lasting, positive impact on the world.

CONCLUSION

"From Zero to Profit" encapsulates a journey that is both inspiring and practical, illustrating the trajectory of building something substantial out of nothing. This progression, often characterized by resilience, strategy, and adaptability, culminates in the achievement of profitability. In this thousand-word conclusion, I'll delve into the key themes and takeaways from this transformative journey.

The path from zero to profit is a testament to the entrepreneurial spirit's vitality, where an initial idea, however small, transforms into a viable business. It is a journey marked by hurdles, challenges, and a continuous learning curve. One of the fundamental lessons gleaned from this progression is the importance of perseverance. The journey from inception to profitability rarely unfolds without setbacks or moments of doubt. It requires an unwavering commitment to the vision despite obstacles.

Flexibility and adaptability are other indispensable traits on this journey. Entrepreneurs often encounter unforeseen circumstances, market shifts, or technological advancements that demand quick pivots. Being adaptable, ready to reevaluate strategies and pivot direction when necessary, can be the defining factor between stagnation and progress.

A crucial aspect of this journey is the significance of a well-defined strategy. Moving from zero to profit necessitates meticulous planning, a thorough understanding of market dynamics, and a clear roadmap. Setting attainable short-term goals while keeping sight of the long-term vision allows for measured progress and a sense of accomplishment along the way.

Furthermore, the importance of resilience in the face of failure cannot be overstated. Failures and setbacks are inevitable companions on this journey. They provide invaluable lessons, shaping the entrepreneur and the business for future success. Embracing failure as a stepping stone to growth and not a roadblock is a distinguishing characteristic of successful ventures.

Building a sustainable and profitable business also requires a keen focus on customer needs and market trends. Understanding the target audience, their pain points, and providing innovative solutions sets the foundation for success. A customer-centric approach fosters loyalty, propelling growth through word-of-mouth referrals and repeat business.

Moreover, the journey from zero to profit is not merely about financial gains. It encompasses personal growth and development. The skills acquired, the resilience honed, and the networks established contribute significantly to an entrepreneur's growth. This journey fosters qualities such as leadership, adaptability, and a knack for problem-solving that extend beyond the business realm.

Collaboration and building a strong team are pivotal elements in achieving profitability. No venture succeeds solely on the efforts of a single individual. It requires a cohesive team sharing the same vision, contributing their expertise, and working synergistically towards common goals. Effective delegation, fostering a positive work culture, and nurturing talent are essential for sustained success.

Embracing innovation and staying abreast of technological advancements are vital for staying competitive in today's dynamic business landscape. The ability to leverage new technologies and trends can provide a competitive edge, opening new avenues for growth and profitability.

From a broader perspective, the journey from zero to profit is a testament to the human spirit's capacity for creation and innovation. It underscores the importance of entrepreneurship in driving economic growth and fostering innovation in society. The entrepreneurial journey embodies the ethos of taking risks, challenging the status quo, and creating value for oneself and others.

In conclusion, the odyssey from zero to profit encapsulates a myriad of experiences, challenges, and triumphs. It demands resilience, strategic planning, adaptability, and a customer-centric approach. The journey is not solely about financial gain but encompasses personal growth, innovation, and societal impact. It stands as a testament to the entrepreneurial spirit's resilience and ability to transform ideas into profitable enterprises. Ultimately, it is a journey that celebrates human ingenuity, determination, and the pursuit of turning dreams into reality.